SPECTACULAR SHIPS

Collector Card

SPECTACULAR SHIPS

Collector Card

SPECTACULAR SHIPS

Collector Card

SPECTACULAR SHIPS

Collector Card

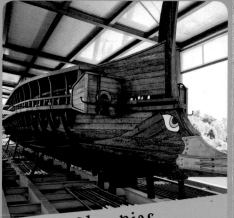

Olympias

A modern replica of a trireme from Ancient Greece.

SCORE

LENGTH: 121 ft. (36.9m)		2
PEOPLE ONBOARD: 205		3
TOP SPEED: 10.6 mph (17km/h)		3
DEADLINESS: fighters and archers		3

Santa Maria

A replica of the flagship of the explorer Christopher Columbus.

SCORE

LENGTH: 62 ft. (19m)		1
PEOPLE ONBOARD: about 50		2
TOP SPEED: 9mph (15km/h)		1
DEADLINESS: a few cannons		4

HMS Victory

Admiral Nelson's warship from the Battle of Trafalgar.

SCORE

LENGTH: 226 ft. (69m)		3
PEOPLE ONBOARD: 850		5
TOP SPEED: 13.7 mph (22km/h)		5
DEADLINESS: 104 cannons		6

R.MS Titanic

The unsinkable ship that sank on its maiden voyage.

SCORE

LENGTH: 883 ft. (269m)		7
PEOPLE ONBOARD: 3327		8
TOP SPEED: 27 mph (44km/h)		9
DEADLINESS: some pistols		2

It's all about…

SPECTACULAR SHIPS

KINGFISHER
NEW YORK

KINGFISHER
LONDON & NEW YORK

Copyright © Macmillan Publishers International Ltd 2016
Published in the United States by Kingfisher,
175 Fifth Ave., New York, NY 10010
Kingfisher is an imprint of Macmillan Children's Books, London

Distributed in the U.S. and Canada by Macmillan,
175 Fifth Ave., New York, NY 10010

Library of Congress Cataloging-in-Publication data
has been applied for.

Series editor: Sarah Snashall
Series design: Anthony Hannant (LittleRedAnt)
Written by Sarah Snashall

ISBN 978-0-7534-7289-7

Kingfisher books are available for special promotions
and premiums. For details contact: Special Markets
Department, Macmillan, 175 Fifth Ave.,
New York, NY 10010.

For more information, please visit
www.kingfisherbooks.com

Printed in China

9 8 7 6 5 4 3 2 1

1TR/0616/WKT/UG/128

Picture credits
The Publisher would like to thank the following for permission to reproduce their material.
Top = t; Bottom = b; Center = c; Left = l; Right = r
Cover Shutterstock/E.G.Pors; Back cover Shutterstock/Jeanette Dieti; Page 1 Shutterstock/
E.G.Pors; 2–3, 16–17, 30–31 Shutterstock/bcampbell65; 4 Shutterstock/Silia Photo;
5 Shutterstock/OzPhotoguy; 6–7 Shutterstock/Ronnie Chua; 7 Alamy/Ancient Art &
Architecture Collection; 8 Alamy/Pictorial Press; 8–9 Shutterstock/Joseph Sohm;
10 Shutterstock/Patryk Kosmider; 11 Shutterstock/Everett Historical; 12 Bridgeman/National
Geographic Creative/Robert McGinnes; 13t Getty/Peter Ptschelinzew; 13b Getty/Hulton
Archive/Stringer; 14 Alamy/World History Archive; 15 Alamy/Chris Hellier; 15t Picture Desk/
Chris Deakes; 17t Shutterstock/Victor Maschek; 17b Alamy/imageBROKER; 18–19 Getty/
Photo12; 19t Getty/Scott Polar Research Institute, University of Cambrige; 20–21 Alamy/
nidpor; 21t Corbis/Ralph White; 22–23 Photobucket; 23t, 25 MoD Crown; 24 koreaonthego;
26 Kyle D Gahlau; 27 victor-ny; 27t US Navy/Zack Baddorf; 28 Alamy/aerial-photos.com;
29t Juliet Marine Systems.
Cards: Front tl Flickr/John Chouvardas; tr Shutterstock/Joseph Sohm; bl Shutterstock/Colin
Hutchings; Back tl Shutterstock/Altormmfoto; tr Alamy/GL Archive; bl Flickr/US Navy;
br Flickr/Kees torn.

Front cover: A fully loaded container ship leaves port with the help of a tugboat.

CONTENTS

For your free audio download go to
www.panmacmillan.com/audio/
SpectacularShips **or** goo.gl/5G9Dkn
Happy listening!

From log to liner

Long ago, people built boats by hollowing out logs or weaving plant parts together. Since those early days, we have built bigger boats and better ships: ships for transporting goods, ships for trading, ships for invading, and ships for adventure.

Vikings traveled in their longships from Scandinavia to Africa, Greenland, and Canada.

Famous for:	world's largest passenger ship
Length:	1188 ft. (362m)
Capacity:	6296 passengers and 2000+ crew
Maiden voyage:	December 1, 2010

Enormous cruise ships carry thousands of passengers. They are like floating towns.

FACT ...

Viking chiefs and nobles were buried in ships filled with luxury goods.

Early traders

In ancient times, the Greeks, Romans, Phoenicians, and Chinese sailed strong wooden ships with sails and oars. They used them to both trade and fight with their neighbors.

FACT ...

Chinese junks had rudders and compasses 1000 years before ships in Europe did.

Triremes were fast warships used by the Ancient Greeks and Romans. They had sails and up to 170 oarsmen who rowed for six hours a day.

Chinese junks, similar to those used by the Ancient Chinese, are still in use today.

Voyages of discovery

As ships became stronger and could travel farther, adventurers went on voyages of discovery to look for exotic spices, new lands, and fame. Their ships had large square sails to catch the wind and cross the oceans faster. There was room onboard for about 80 men and 20 cannons.

The English explorer Sir Francis Drake sailed the *Golden Hind* around the world.

FACT ...

When the explorer Christopher Columbus arrived in the Americas on October 12, 1492, he thought he had arrived in the East Indies.

This ship is a replica of the *Santa Maria*, in which Christopher Columbus first sailed to the Americas.

Beware of pirates!

By the 1600s, the oceans were full of
large galleons carrying gold from the
Americas and spices from the East
Indies. These were rich pickings for
pirates! Pirates would attack ships, steal
their goods, and often kill the sailors.

Spanish galleons were powerful ships
with five masts.

Pirates flew the Jolly Roger, or a plain black flag, to frighten the crew of other ships.

FACT ...

Pirates often shared the treasure fairly among themselves and voted on who should be captain.

The pirate Blackbeard sailed a ship called the *Queen Anne's Revenge*. It carried 40 cannons.

Life onboard

Could you survive a life on the seas? If you ran away to sea 400 years ago, you might regret it quite soon. You would sleep wherever you could find space. Food would be salted meat and dry ship's biscuits—perhaps filled with weevils! You would be at sea for months without washing or changing your clothes.

Without fresh food to eat, people were in danger of catching a disease called scurvy.

FACT...

Spanish sailors visiting the West Indies saw locals sleeping in hammocks. Soon sailors started using them onboard ships.

Each ship had a surgeon who cut hair and amputated diseased limbs.

Leaving home

In 1620, 102 "pilgrims" left Plymouth, England, on a merchant ship called the *Mayflower* to start a new life in America. Since then, many thousands have traveled on ships to start new lives abroad. From 1820 to 1920, 18 million people sailed from Europe to settle in America.

Pilgrims board the *Mayflower* in Plymouth, England.

ABERDEEN &
COMMONWEALTH LINE
THE FASTEST LINE TO AUSTRALIA

ONE CLASS
SERVICE
VIA
SUEZ CANAL
& COLOMBO

It took 35 to 40 days
to sail to Australia
in the 1920s.

FACT ...

For two hundred years, the British Government
sent prisoners to prison villages in America and
then Australia. Most people chose to stay there.

15

Shipwreck!

The ocean is a dangerous place. Over the centuries, ships have been sunk by whales, waves, and rocks. Most ships were broken up by the ocean but some sank into the mud, waiting to be discovered by divers.

A diver explores the wreck of the *Wallaurie*, in the Bahamas.

The Swedish ship the *Vasa* sank in 1628 on its first voyage. In 1961, it was brought to the surface.

Shipwrecks can tell us about life onboard the ship.

An icy adventure

Fridtjof Nansen designed a very strong boat for his unsuccessful attempt to sail to the North Pole. The *Fram* was trapped in the ice for three years but the crew were comfortable: the *Fram* had an insulated hull, an electric generator, plenty of food, and a piano.

The *Fram* had three masts and an engine. It was shallow and wide to withstand the ice.

Ernest Shackleton's ship, the *Endurance*, was trapped for 10 months before it was crushed by the ice.

SPOTLIGHT: Fram

Famous for:	polar expedition ship
Length:	127 ft. 7in. (38.9m)
Capacity:	16 men
Maiden voyage:	1893

FACT ...

The Norwegian explorer Roald Amundsen used the *Fram* when he went to the South Pole.

Titanic

The luxury passenger liner *Titanic* left Southampton for New York on April 10, 1912. It had many magnificent rooms but it did not have enough lifeboats. On April 14, the *Titanic* hit an iceberg and sank. A total of 1500 people lost their lives.

The *Titanic* had two huge steam engines and could travel at 27 mph (44km/h).

SPOTLIGHT: Titanic

Famous for:	hitting an iceberg
Length:	883 ft. (269m)
Capacity:	2435 passengers plus 892 crew
Maiden voyage:	1912

FACT ...

Many of the *Titanic's* lifeboats were launched half full, and only 710 people were saved.

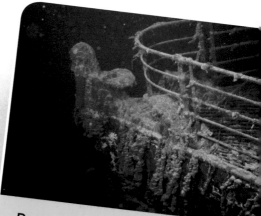

Part of the wreck of the *Titanic*.

Hard work

Today, the oceans are filled with hard-working ships. Thousands of huge freighters cross the world's shipping lanes carrying goods and oil. There are also icebreakers, fishing trawlers, research ships, and ships that lay internet cables on the ocean floor.

FACT ...

Supertanker *Knock Nevis* was longer than the height of the Empire State Building in New York.

Icebreakers are strong enough to break through ice. The ship's hull is shaped to push the ice out of the way.

SPOTLIGHT: Knock Nevis

Famous for:	longest and heaviest ship
Length:	1503 ft. (458m)
Capacity:	622,544 tons (564,763 tonnes) oil
Maiden voyage:	1979

Ships at war

The toughest ships have always been warships. These ships have the biggest guns, the fastest speeds, and the strongest hulls. Early warships were built of thick oak and armed with cannons. Today, warships have iron hulls, big guns, and torpedoes.

The Korean turtle ship was armed with a sulfur gas thrower, iron spikes, and cannons.

SPOTLIGHT: HMS Victory

Famous for:	Battle of Trafalgar
Length:	226 ft. (69m)
Capacity:	about 850 sailors and soldiers
Maiden voyage:	1765

HMS *Victory*, the flagship of Britain's Admiral Nelson, had 104 cannons.

HMS *Argyll* is a very fast-moving warship. The ship patrols the Caribbean looking for drug smugglers.

Above and below

In modern wars, destroyers can launch missiles at a target hundreds of miles away. Fighter planes, surveillance planes, and helicopters can take off and land on aircraft carriers. Under the ocean, submarines spy on enemy ships.

About 3000 people live and work onboard an aircraft carrier.

A nuclear submarine can stay underwater until the food runs out.

FACT ...

USS *Triton* was the first submarine to travel around the world underwater.

SPOTLIGHT: USS Nautilus

Famous for:	first nuclear submarine
Length:	321 ft. (98m)
Capacity:	105 submariners
Maiden voyage:	1954

571

Ships of the future

What will ships look like in the future? Some will be bigger, some will be faster, and others will save fuel by using solar panels and sails, or by floating on a cushion of gas or bubbles.

The deck of the *Tûranor PlanetSolar*, the world's largest solar-powered boat, is covered with 809 solar panels.

Is it a boat? Is it a plane? The *GHOST* marine platform is a stealth ship that moves on gas bubbles to travel faster.

FACT ...

The *GHOST* marine platform has been designed to attack modern-day pirates.

The hull of this Swedish stealth ship, the *Helsingborg*, is made of carbon fiber and vinyl to make it difficult to detect.

GLOSSARY

aircraft carrier A warship with a large flat area from which small aircraft take off and land.

compass An instrument that points to north and can be used to navigate.

cruise liner A large ship for vacationers which travels from port to port.

destroyer A small, heavily armed ship that protects larger warships.

freighter A ship designed to carry goods.

galleon A large sailing ship with square sails used for war and trade.

hull The main body of the ship (not including the masts).

mast A tall, upright post that carries the sails.

nuclear submarine An underwater vessel that is powered by a nuclear reactor.

pirate A robber who attacks ships from another ship or boat.

rigging A system of ropes that supports a ship's mast and operates the sails.

rudder A movable flat piece of wood or metal that sticks out from the bottom and back of a ship and is used to steer it.

solar panel A flat plate that converts energy from the sun into another form of energy, such as electricity.

spice A food flavoring grown in hot parts of the world.

supertanker An enormous oil tanker.

surveillance Watching something closely, often without being seen.

tanker A ship that carries large amounts of oil.

torpedo An underwater missile.

trireme An Ancient Greek or Roman ship with three rows of oars.

INDEX

SPECTACULAR SHIPS

Collector Card

SPECTACULAR SHIPS

Collector Card

SPECTACULAR SHIPS

Collector Card

SPECTACULAR SHIPS

Collector Card

Allure of the Sea

The largest cruise ship in the world has 24 elevators.

SCORE

LENGTH: 1188 ft. (362m)	9
PEOPLE ONBOARD: 8296	10
TOP SPEED: 26 mph (42km/h)	8
DEADLINESS:	0

The famous German battleship from World War II.

SCORE

LENGTH: 823 ft. (251m)	6
PEOPLE ONBOARD: 2065	7
TOP SPEED: 35 mph (56km/h)	10
DEADLINESS: 62 huge guns	8

USS Nimitz aircraft carrier

A huge nuclear-powered aircraft carrier that can hold 90 aircraft.

SCORE

LENGTH: 1089 ft. (332m)	8
PEOPLE ONBOARD: 5680	9
TOP SPEED: 35 mph (56km/h)	10
DEADLINESS: 90 fighter jets	10

MSC Oscar

The largest container ship in the world can carry 19,224 containers.

SCORE

LENGTH: 1299 ft. (396m)	10
PEOPLE ONBOARD: 35	1
TOP SPEED: 26 mph (42km/h)	8
DEADLINESS:	0